Praise for Pathways

In the opus *Pathways: Walking Through Creation*, author Brenda Asterino seems not only to have covered Earth but the universe too! That below us, that above us, and so much of what is in between constitute her writing pad. From as early as 1954 when so many thought so much of the world could be compartmentalized to 2020-2021 when the pandemic and protests awakened so many to our interdependence and lack of equity and inclusion, the poet has been recording her thoughts, feelings on innumerable subjects, some of which we surely have thought similarly and others that might not cross our minds in a lifetime. Much is fascinating here. And though you may choose different paths, it helps us all to know that so many paths exist, that a variety of these paths can help and not impede humankind at a time when we need much help and guidance in countless ways.

You won't regret allowing *Pathways* to lead you up and down paths familiar and unfamiliar as you read the book. You'll not forget some of these paths and may indeed choose to investigate some further and perhaps forge a path or few of your own.

—Georgia S. McDade, Author of *Outside the Cave and Observations and Revelations: Stories, Sketches, and Essays*

This is an insightful collection that covers the scope of the micro-connections that ground, and bind us in thought, and the meta-external challenges that, with hope and perseverance, can inspire us together in action.

—AC Palmer

If you want to hold hands with the stars, unknown horizons, and the world of possibilities while firmly living in the practical realities of life, this profoundly intimate sharing is for you.

Brenda Asterino masterfully walks the reader through the complexities of life as she learns and grows from her joys, disappointments, tragedies, and insights.

Brenda's thoughts through the years provide a backward glance at changing social and cultural mores as her own personal development emerges, then plunks us right in the middle of a one-hundred-year pandemic.

The scope of her sharing is tremendous. Brenda covers sixty years and touches on significant human reflections that help the reader ponder their life journey: why am I here, what have I learned, how can I help make things better?

As I concluded my prolonged and deliberative reading of *Pathways: Walking Through Creation*, I found myself asking the question—"what are my next steps?"

—Dixie Adair Budke, Ph.D.

Pathways

WALKING THROUGH CREATION

Brenda M. Asterino

Pathways

Walking Through Creation

Brenda M. Asterino

Sidekick Press
Bellingham, Washington

ISBN 978-1-7365358-4-4
LCCN 2021913163

Published by:
Sidekick Press
2950 Newmarket Street
Suite 101-329
Bellingham, WA 98226

Cover Design by Spoken Designs www.spokendesigns.com

Dedication

To all who study
that which is about their feet
and to those who gaze at the stars.
Never stop reaching out to each other.

I live on the ancestral lands and waters of the Coast Salish Sea Peoples who have called this place home and cared for it since time immemorial. Pledging to work for reconciliation, I regret the harm done to them by the settler culture.

Contents

From a Body of Nature

Winged Blessings

I remember butterflies.
Dozens on an August evening,
Dropping to the warm concrete
Before the gingerbread front porch.

I was ten or twelve years old
And with quiet, gentle movement,
A humble "i" would join them,
Bowing in supplication.

Tiny feet did grace my arms,
Befriend my shoulder, kissed my hair.
Fragile brown-orange flutters
Were experienced . . .
Now, gone.

The Experience of Movement

Movement is:
Stretching out arm,
Pushing a circular gesture,
Testing shoulder's range of motion.

Micro-movements in fingers,
Wrist sets up opposing action.

Waves and circles with spiral support.

Grounding, mind field moves against
And down lumbar and sacral vertebrae.

Feel sitz (the bones in your tush) bones
Against padded chair seat.

Feet chakras open,
With connection to Mother
Breathing up earth energies
Heaviness in legs and warming up pelvis.

Solar plexus quiets and realigns.
Awareness shifts to bone and sinew—

Muscle, fascia, skin as organ.
Mind and body connects.
Spirit flows in
To act out.

Automatic great breath inspires
Deep into lungs,
With joy leaping
As heart frees larger than self.

Shoulder girdle raises—
Releases making space for surge to throat,
Shoulders, arms, and hands.

Ancient veils unfolding,
Lifting in an opening lotus dance.

Concurrently, spontaneously,
Without need for activity of thought,
Energy nourishes bone,
Enriching blood.

Energy and breath feed blood, body, and brain.
Integration of chest expands
Into accord with pelvic and shoulder girdle rhythm.

In response to oneness of the moment.
A long low "O" sound vibrates
And punctuates matter creating space—
A wormhole to the spine
Where kundalini snakes in vibrant color
Undulates from feet to crown
With eye forming blue to violet,
Greeted at spreading arachnoid process

By lubricating fluid bathing brain cells abundantly.

Shifts of color with silver undertones
Shoot through cellular landscapes
Brightening synapses to the atomic level . . .

And biochemistry is changed.

Musings on the Macrocosm

From the darkness of Not-nothing . . .

Full of Itself circling,
Pierced through by the light.
Sparking motion with notion . . .

Looking back on Not-nothing.

Drawn through Itself to the dawn
Of Now.

Elementals

What are you really?

Are you elf?
Imagination longs to know.

Are you a spark of the divine?

Are you
Neutrino or water sprite?
Are you quark or God-stuff?

Before the Before Life . . .

The mix before me winds and twirls and flicks:
An accident of birth;
A hybrid of time and forces,
Making a symphony,
A harmony of earth;
Fire, water, and pressure.

As a counter-rhythm occurs washing
Against and making friction,
Fractionalizing
With new combinations.

Permutations cavort to polarize
And display rhythmic grace
Lineage of types within growing
Subtle factories
Of lightning or forces unknown.

Might there be a kiss of pressured passion?
A hug of lathered burst,
A sweep of grueling wind or
A pinch of baking sun?

A tide turns, new combinations surge
To a chain that merges;
An edge of residual ruminating rinse
And of slippery slime.

Does it gain a place, a congregate space?
Does it ultimately lead to
Brain or bone, sinew or muscle, hinged jaw?
Machination of cell?

Does the rhythm abide to percolate?
Embracing molecule
For an act of reproduction?
Shall we repose or replicate . . .
which makes life?

The Wind

Oh, wind,
I love your storms,
Your every little breeze.

I feel
You going through my hair
And hear you whistling
Through the trees.

I join
Your every howling sound
That you alone can make.

And watch ripples in the stream,
Through the fields
And on the lake.

I love
The way you bend the trees
And dust the cobwebs
From the eaves.

I see
You sweep the streets,
And prance with
All the leaves.

Nodding

Hazy, pasty, darkening sky.
Blanketing the light of day.
Softens and slows my breath.

Away I slide
Into that yawning sky
Thickened with unshed rain,
That weighs down my eyelids.

An Act of Bee at Notre Dame

Beloved Lady
My heart is tattered
There's too much deranged
One more thing shattered.

I am weary
With my worldly care
Prove to me, please
That you are still there.

I looked into fire
All flame and all smoke
Terror consumed me
Fearful, I choked.

But . . .
"Bees have returned,"
The internet said
Rooftop hives alive
Removed all my dread.

Gratitude, Joy will
Release this dismay
The Truth never changed
I looked the wrong way.

Cycles continue
Justice is real
When fearless acts
Of love are revealed.

Is love not faith?
The faith to believe?
That all is not lost,
Even bees perceived.

Sacred Beloved,
It's so from the start
All life at all times
Is found in an art.

Please act on it—
We play our own parts.
All life for all times
Is in our own hearts.

Autumn Cake

Combining dusky blue clouds
With foggy mornings
Is a late summer confection.

Blend brightening swaths
Falling, turning leaves
Make autumnal concoctions.

Whipping between the dawn
And the lengthening of nights
Swirl October festivals.

Mix what's hot, add what's cold
Spices old and new
Fires are lit in homes and heart.

Garnish with our laughter
Serve with cyclic joy
In homes of family and friends.

What Glory the Nature of Woman

Lichen shadowing
Accentuating
As green multiplies
On dull grey bark.
And skipping across
To the tops of the cliffs
Of the carved expansion.
Changing size and shape
With growth and age.
Always giving,
Providing food or
Sheltering
For other life.

Women, like those trees
That never stop changing,
Are always expanding,
Renewing, in different ways.

The ultimate betrayal of ego
Is to give
Over
To life.

As with raw clay
The potential is the
Ultimate goal.
And maybe why the feminine
Was worshipped long ago.

Without submitting
To life
There is only a death inside the skin,
Building walls within
And without our lives,
And in regard to
Our influence
In the lives of others.

Women are the juxtaposition.
That flexibility of change
Of hard and soft
Sweet and salty
Give and take.

What glory,
To be born
A woman.

The Sea of Me

Sea sensations
brood within me.
Moon-rocked ocean water
serves the minute
and the monstrous,
modeling many life templates
within the same space
at the same time.
Does cradling a baby
mimic that movement and
integrate function that needs
lymphatic stimulation
and nervous system soothing?

Inside out becomes outside in
as we travel from the complexity
of molecular sea without
to the bag of living water
walking about.
Pulling ourselves above the water
is self-delusion.
It doesn't stop the sight
of graceful frond illusion
like breeze inciting the brain
to make a physical partnership.

We move toward and in the water
as if we crave it, bit by bit.

An ancient memory?
What reminds us to reach
for air and land?
What is our future
as oceans reclaim earth?

If sentience came before the sea,
does it ride the waves
or watch the flow?
Does interdependency
prove being able to know?

Life continually blooms
in Earth's liquid realms
in a constant process of patterns
that are planet-wide.
There are no boundaries
in this space.
The order of chaos
is without border.

At the swell of gestation,
the future yearns
and spreads
weaving threads in
every direction
from that auspicious well.

Surprise Delivery from Covid

Bubbles of memories
Come forth from the rubble
Of old dictates for survival
And move on.

Fragments of old times
And older ways grasp
And squeeze my heart
When I'm lost and awash
In self-pity.

Then, an action turns
And opens to radiance
Lending focus
For redefining
Connections.

I am without remorse
or duty.
But doing daily
For a tomorrow
That is good.

Covid Vaccination

Sniffle, snorfel, snuffle
Painful muscles to bones,
Thick breath
Faulty faculties

Ranting wracking woofing
Flimsy feverish foment
Astride a rocking steed.

It stops when it stops.

It was done
For community
Not for me.

From Another Time . . .

Dazzle me, call to me,
Break me to heal.
Break loose from the snare,
What else can I feel?

Shadows move with me
Release them to ground.
As time opens up
For love to abound.

The center of spiral
Is with us right now.

Long time ago, cut off at my knees
Broke all our minds
As they killed off the bees.

Circle of my hand, roll of my hips
Flow forth the love from my heart with a kiss
Nothing is lost, wholeness is gained
As the power from feet rises again.

So twirl and swirl,
Dance through the dream
To knit up the time
So we all can be seen.

Sweep out the cobwebs
Ache loose the pain.
Sing praise to all Goodness
Without any shame.

The dance never stops,
The dance never slows,
We might change the beat
But never
The . . . heat.

Dreaming the Body

Car accident,
Long hospital stay.
Locked in a bed
Right limb won't walk.
No cooperation
Between thigh, leg, and foot.

Over two weeks,
Nothing changed or moved.
Only fainting.
After lots of effort
A dream came in the night.

I was walking.
Then full out running.
Felt dream movements;
From muscle to my bone
There was joy of running.

Sweet memory
Woke nervous system.
Made me able
To stand and coordinate.
Mind's dream is physical.

For Consciousness' Sake

A Plan

Believe and hold to dreams
For tomorrow's made for you.
Believe and weave your schemes
And learn to follow through.
For tomorrow's made for you.

Learn to love through caring
And love to learn to grow.
Mistakes will have no bearing
On tomorrow's right to show
That tomorrow's made for you.

Think on what, and will be
And know that it is true.
Place it in your mind to see,
So the future has a cue,
That tomorrow's made for you.

Believe that you've a right
For tomorrow to be new.
Believe and hold on tight.
It's all up to you to do,
For tomorrow's made for you.

The Long Gaze

I sit on the beach
And look out upon the bay
And farther.
At rest and still lingering,
Wondering at the distance,
Marveling at the vastness.

The long gaze,
Out beyond the next island
Goes on for miles,
Sparking an inspiration that
Fills my lungs.
It takes me to places between
The space of this
Lifetime and . . . others.

Felt without thought;
Sensed with scenes
And stray feelings
Within growing awareness.

Is all time in the same place?

I turn a degree to left
Or to the right,
And other worlds await.

Ancient Stones

In the daybreak,
As breeze ruffles spruce
Hear crows caw "frozen" time.
Smell the breathy sigh
Of those waiting for the thaw.

As mist crouches
Upon paradise,
See almost, but not-quite
Timeless faces torn
From island community.

Some do mistake
Stuck as spiritual.
Mired feelings, drugged numb
Lies are not healing.
Truth and Justice on the drums!

Names framed by cries,
Bones of the Mother
Bleed for the children gone.
Groans reshape the land.
Searing eyes flash vibrant flame.
Stones shine as passion reigns.

Re-Member-ing Makes a Better World

Hey, You—I'm talking to You!
Do you remember
Playing with your whole heart?

Did you have fantastic daydreams,
Travels to exotic places?
Did you build cities for toys?

How often did you fly
In dreams or with a towel as cape?
How awesome was nature?

Remember and imagine.
Recreate, re-create, co-create.
Write a song,
A play.

Making a better world
Calls for playing wholeheartedly.

Especially if we play together.

Dragonflies

From shadowy depths rise the
Dragonflies of time,
With laboring wings shun the
Caverns of my mind.

What useless time is spent
In darkened alleyways,
Constructive energy on black
And long gone days.

Regrets can only make my spirit
Fold and die.

So, release and let go.
Allow dragons to fly.

Thankfulness

Thank God
For the gift
Of New Life in each day.

I bow down to God.

Bow down to the Power.
Bow down to the Light.
Bow down to Authority
That tells you what's Right!

:)

Then, I'll make a left turn,
That is right!

And I'll dance with the Goddess of the Light and the Dark
And I'll sing of Justice and Truth.
And Together we'll dance and we'll sing
And we'll laugh
In the Joy of All Creation.

Darkness

Darkness comes to all.
Invisible in all life patterns
Because the light
Makes shadow
And is too bright
For it to be seen.

Darkness reminds us
We're never promised a rose garden.
Deep in soft petals
It's hidden.
It's not bidden,
So darkness resides.

Silently it comes
Gradually spreading fathomless wings
Blotting our sense of direction.
So, in contrast
It brings forth the light.

Some experience it plaguing our lives
As it crushes dreams
Taking what's precious through death
It will swallow us
And spit us back out.

Darkness comes to us
Until we feel it, hold it, know it
For what it is.
Its power
For its control
Leaves us as we let go.

And, then, Darkness will come again.

Waves

Waves of joy, liquid emotion,
From a source unseen.

Flowing and swirling in sensory delight,
Infinity beckons, as I humbly stare.

Thought forms that coalesce in air
Wink in and out, leaving me bare,
Shattering boundaries that were once so complete.

Grasping for words,
Hope has returned.

When physical senses only serve to deceive,
The heart that is true will help you perceive.

A STARtle

What star did you come from?

Or did the star come to you?

Was it a spark of awareness?

Was it a lightning bolt?

Did your inner sight enlighten you?

Did the enlightenment grow to inner sight?

Are you a five-pointed star awakening
Changing to New Earth awareness?

Are you a six-pointed star
Balancing and spinning into integration?

Were you startled into recognition
Of who you are and who you want to be?

Are your golden feathers illuminated
By the star that shines from your single eye?

Does your mind perceive
Your golden worth?

Undefined
(Traumatic Brain Injury)

Continuing care hospital bed.
Growing anxiety when mind has any clarity.

Repeating need to check purse, to handle makeup.

Send for the nurse.

Unable to be erect or walk the space—to make the twentieth
search for mirror, lipstick, mascara.

Feeling through every pocket, over and over again.
Gone with the rolls of the car.

Finding only shattered glass.

Makeup gone, anxiety grows,
as if face cannot be defined without it.
Filling up with confusion.

Not knowing yet that my life is no longer defined.

I, who is known to me, who is no longer.

Awakening from a Dream

Awakening from a dream
Not quite all the way
Confusion takes the lead
Hoping for a better day.

A moment changed the world
Always lost in time
'Cause there's no guarantees
On this journey of the mind.

There's something deep inside
That beats and breaks and longs
Struggling in the silence
To play half-forgotten songs.

Enjoying where you are
Helps to redefine
There's nothing incomplete
Within God's own space and time.

People hurt, people leave
Find those who understand
Got to trust in angels
And it helps to hold a hand.

What comes through our hearts?
What are we to know?
Did we learn and love enough?
Have we touched another soul?

East Joins West

November, Washington, D.C.
Traditional Tibetan Practitioners
Meet Western Doctors
Presiding was H.H. the Dalai Lama
Panels:
Traditional Tibetan Medicine and
Current Clinical and Scientific Research.
Methodologies.
Mind-body Relationships.
Mental Health.
Death and Dying
Environmental Issues.
Spiritual Teachings of
Medicine Buddha and
Bon Po perspective.
Bridges were made.

Reunion of East and West

Eagles have ancient memories
Of magnificent dragons.
They cry the sound
Of timeless ages
Brought forth from harmonic heartbeat
And benevolent breath.

While rainbows form pillars
Between earth and the heavens,
Dawning to a new doorway
Illuminated by ancestral love.

Pondering the Divine Feminine

From oceanic soup,
Climbing the Tower of Magdala,
Through the Spiral of Wisdom,
Reaching for the Hand of the Beloved.

Experience a quickening mind from within
Compassion.

Resist not the caverns of the mind,
But fill with majestic breath.

Shining light, Human Be-ing.
We stand upright and grasp our birthright.

We are who we are with open hands;
Channeling enthusiasm,
Making heaven on earth,
Empowered as children,
Chosen to play, accept, enjoy, release.

Am of I, Am that is.
Embracing through glowing countenance.

Drumming our beat
Moving everything to oneness of everything
Within timelessness of community.

All that ever was will forever be.
Showing our birthright with open hand.
Take into your heart new creation.

Prodigals

All is not lost,
For the party is waiting.

There have been mistakes;
Unskilled labor,
Immaturity,
Losing our way.

Commitments are needed;
Of faith, Of responsibility.
All is not lost.

The feast is being prepared.
The party is waiting.

Yes

Because I said, Yes!

The Hypnotist said, "Let's start."
I said, Yes.

The hypnotist said,
"Count down deeper."
I went deeper, and felt weightless and drifting.

The hypnotist said,
"Count up, go to spirit."
I headed toward the light and felt at peace.

The hypnotist said,
"What do you see?"
I see threads of silver, gold, platinum, and rose pink.

"What else do you see?"
I see the lights of many colors
moving along the strings of metal.

"How many are there?"
Too many to count,
too beautiful not to feel like
I might burst open.

"What else do you see?"
I thought I saw straight, metallic streams
but now I see they curve and circle and spiral.

"What are the colors of the lights?"
All the colors of the rainbow and more . . .
going on forever, farther than the eye can see.

"What do you see now? Can you get closer?"
They are alive and they come to me and circle and spiral
around me and dance and I want to leap with them in Joy.

And all because I said, "Yes"!

Human Culture

A Culture of Choices

Are we in the culture of humanity?
Or the culture of mankind?
Or the culture of capitalism?
Or the culture of community?

Are we in a culture of growth?
Or a culture of disease?
Or a culture of hierarchy?
Or a culture of equality?

Are we in a culture of justice?
Justice for whom?

Are we the culture builders?
Can we start anew?
It's our choice.

Sitting on a Porch Step

Sitting on a porch step,
Not even middle age,
Weeping for friends lost in just one day.

Good friends and longtime friends,
Sometimes even close friends.
Weeping for lives going separate ways.

Don't want to just stand still,
Although, I'm not sure why.
Weeping for the change, must do or die?

Moving up, moving out,
Just plain moving along,
Weeping turns from tears into a sigh.

Her Love

Hearing the slights of ignorance,
Feeling the icy cut of exclusion,
She has known the hurt of hate.

She holds her focus
To remember:
Rocking her baby;
The sweetness of her baby's breath;
The strength of his tiny grip;
The softness of his creamy brown skin.

The Growl of Freedom (Navy Growlers)

Arrogantly grasping
As owning the sky
Pollute water, land
out of sight.

Dominant rasping
Against body and mind
Claiming everything
as their right.

Caesar of air,
Profit Alliance,
While demanding
our compliance.

Protection becomes
Enslavement at its core.
They growl,
We whimper.

And there's no exit door.

Merry-go-round

Merry-go-round, go up and down.
Riding higher to the sky.
Where are you going? Where am I?
Am I fast or are you slow?
You all glide away the higher I go.
Merry go high, merry go low.

Does his smile go up or down?
Can't always tell on the merry-go-round.
I like the horse with the wild eye.
Too far to touch.
Watch your life pass you by.
Merry goes 'round and up and down.

Merry-go-round, go 'round, go 'round.
Go 'round, the merry-go-round.
If it goes up
Will you forget who was there?
The cycle never stops, no time to compare.
Go 'round, go 'round, the merry-go-round.

Fear

Fear is contagious.

We all feel it.
Our natural fear
Is useful to those who love power.

Controlling fear though culture makes profit.

Controlling fear through politics makes war.

Some say it makes the world safe,
But never does it make the world safe from fear.

How in the World?
Power Paradigms

How in our time
Did we become so unkind?
What in the world do we do?
How can we make
A flow change to a curve
That will serve as a wake-up call?

How many times
Can we give for a world
Most of us see full of lies?
I want to shout!
Do we dare for our world?
To speak up, speak out, and try?

Do we just breathe
And neglect to connect
Taking our breaths 'til we die?

What in the world
Is our love for this world?
How did it come to be priced?
Why did the cost
Of ideas in this world
Grow to be higher than life?

Do hearts of stone
Make us freeze up our souls,
Suppress who we truly are?

Speaking your truth
Takes a gasp for all life
Each voice a new guiding star.

We will connect,
Breaking stone, melting ice,
By reaching out to each other.

Who in the world
Wants to die for whose world?
Let's make the right not to fight.
Light up this Earth.
Put a moon in your heart,
A sun will shine from your eyes.

Why in the world
Have we been in this world?
What if we are something new?
Understanding
Becomes celebrating
A new world for me and you.

We make bridges
Between heaven and hell
By reaching out to each other.

When in the world
Came the blame in our souls
Boring holes in all our passion?
Let's put a stop
Here and now of shaming
Those who value compassion.

Gather with respect.
Listen with empathy.
And forge new community.
The fall from grace will release
And then it's time to heal
With justice in unity.

We will make new
Past, present, and future
By reaching out to each other.

Instant Coffee

Instant coffee's not so bad.
Instant tea's okay, too.
Makes more time inside the day
Makes more time for me and you.

Gonna stop for supper
Gonna make it quick
Heating dinner in the oven
With time for you and me
For instant love.

Turn the dial to do the dishes.
Stop at Frisch's for the kids.
Drop them at the sitter's,
With a hug and kiss
Of instant love.

Get a blow-dry haircut,
Quick-dry color for my nails.
Plastic flower at my neck,
and L*U*V for instant love.

Calvin at the Pizza Place

Around and 'round the floor you're dancing
Laughing faces watching you
Dancing, dancing to the band
No one else is dancing to.

Funny Man
Are you always all alone?
Where's someone to take you home?

You move your hands to tell us stories
In some language we don't know
Moving, moving to the band
Was it different long ago?

Funny Man
Are you always all alone?
Where's someone to take you home?

They give you beer to keep you quiet
Keep you quiet while insane
Drinking, drinking to the band
Happy that they say your name.

Funny Man
Are you always all alone?
Where's someone to take you home?

Discriminate

Beware of magic elf and snappy troll
Benefactor, "helping" Professional.

Jealous of spirit, she spins illusion,
Promoting her worth and making confusion.

Circling the life broken, scared into need,
Psychic vampire sucking a survival bleed.

Assert your own power to break the lie,
It's never too late to spit in her eye.

Connections

I will not die.
Suppression, shame does not keep me down.
Changing me to my core
Does not change my core.

I am who I am;
I will remember who I am.

When I catch my breath,
I will get strength to my spine
And claim again who I am.

The earth will not die
And neither will I.
I AM.

Listen

Listen to what comes
from inside,
from birth.

It is still there.
Did culture teach it
to hide
in shadows?

Hibernating
'til you get woke?

It's waiting
for your search
for self.

Waiting for you
to die
to birth.

Are you ready?

Nah.

Liberty

Escape tyranny of your mind.
Escape suppression of your voice.
Escape possession of your soul.

By excising your mind, your voice,
And feeling the action
From the core of your soul.

Wealth

Ideas make us rich
Facts make us smart
The best prize of all
Is growing more heart.

That Way (Child Trafficking)

She cries, She dies
A little more each day
A little more each time
The man touches her that way
And some hope chokes.

He runs, He fights
As young as seven fair
His toys are left behind
Forced beyond what he can bear
With loss of mind.

They buy, They sell
While owning all they can
And owning people, too
As part of the power plan
'Cause no one tells.

She's old, and bold
She speaks to what she sees
Ears choosing not to hear
Bullies knock her to her knees
Who counts the tears?

He smiles, He speaks
He's learned to act the part
Still twisting from his pain
Somewhere he lost his heart

The pain is bad
It runs from mind to soul
Swaddles in her core
Spirit reaches to be whole

There is no protection
No justice can be seen.
And upon reflection
Why can't we hear the scream?

Tragedy for Two

She seems so discontented.
She feels tragic more than fragile.
She remembers her father
While excusing his actions.
She wants it to be so, so badly,
She's lost her way.

He put his heavy burden
On her slender shoulders.
Now she tries to carry other's burdens
Hoping again to see her father?
To be in his presence
Writing a story fiction.

When it gets too heavy
She strikes out at others
Especially those who love her
And will stand by her
when she suffers the most.
She suffers for one who never was.

She will blame them for her injury.
Like her father did to her.
She won't drop the burden
She won't stop her suffering.
That way of being
Is the only thing in her life,
The only part of her actions
She knows are real.

Diverse Relationships

Lazy Days

Oh, lazy days,
Those slow and hazy days,
When I was crazy
And in love with you.

Pink carnation
And spaghetti-strap dress.
All dreams were large
And handsome, swivel-hipped.

Touching fingers
Stirred my body to yours
Our love was sweet
Soft-cheeked, smelling good.

The time moved slowly
And strength was renewed
When I was crazy
And in love with you.

Stardust

We're all made from clay,
Ash from dying stars,
And from that light that shines
from your eyes.
We all come from the same thrust:
Cosmic rhythms, moonbeams, and stardust.

Amid Covid-19

Making egg salad at kitchen sink.
Slicing warm, naked eggs cupped in hand.

Looking up and out to sunlight
And there was a hummingbird.

Shorter than my little finger.

Hardly wider.

Rust-colored all over with black-masked face
Sipping boldly, precisely from feeder.

Taking time to get his fill.

Country Love

City Noises shake my nerves.
Lovin' words can go unheard,
Which isn't what it's s'pposed to be about.
It's quiet times for us to be
Sharin' secrets made for two
In early morning country honeydew.

Lilies noddin', bees abuzzin'
As we find the shade of day.
All the sounds are whispers saying
Love and nature are in bloom.

Blinding lights in the city rush;
It gets hard to fight the crush.
I want time to watch the sunlight on your hair
Doing what we feel to do,
We find our way together
Inside the greening ways of summer days.

Boo

Older sis grabs up little sis,
Slipping the pacifier into baby's mouth.
Mommy scoops up purse, and Boo,
the middle sister.

Mommy runs from single-story house
to 1950s car.
Arms and legs tumble
into the vehicle.

Mommy's stress becomes
children's strain for
clarity.
Looking, searching
to read faces
and understand tension.

Blackness of night
competes
as three sets of eyes strain.

Car doors slam.
Pacifier sucking becomes louder,
more intense.

Mommy quickly pushes both
locks down
before Daddy reaches for door handle.

He flat-handedly bangs
on car hood, trunk.
Yelling with wild eyes
at the windows.

Mommy's shaky fingers take two,
and then three tries
to insert key and catch ignition.

Tires roll off the driveway.
Boo in the backseat screams
with tears tracing face
and dripping from nose and chin,
"Daddy, Daddy!"

Delicate fingers claw at unyielding glass.

Mommy turns the wheel,
wipes blood from her mouth
with a swipe of one hand,
and heads the car
toward the road
that takes them out of town.

From the rear window,
darkness frames Daddy,
swallowing the house,
and then him.

The deep space inside the car
holds heavy with
moist, snotty sobs.

The car continues on as a little fist
rubs littler eyes.
Exhaustion steals the sobs of the children
and steels the resolve of Mommy.

Young Love

Our fight was a stupid one
Don't you know, I need you, Hon?
I walked out and ran about
As far as I could run
No money in my pockets
Eyes throbbing in their sockets
What can I change to rearrange
That big fight I won?

Life is as empty as my bed
I can't seem to get my head together
The whole world's turned upside down
What happened to the love we'd found?

Walking back through pouring rain,
Thoughts of you whirled in my brain
Getting back I found the hollow sound
Of empty rooms.
No warmth comes from memories
With you went the best of me
Cold feet under freezing sheet
In the cool of the moon.

Life is as empty as my bed.
I can't seem to get my head together.
The whole world's turned upside down.
What happened to the love we'd found?

I got up to make some toast.
Blurry eyes make out a ghost.
The pain comes back and then I lack
The strength to carry on.

I don't know how I've survived,
Times goes on and I'm alive.
Movement becomes the thing to be done
'til the pain is gone.

Life is as empty as my bed.
I can't seem to get my head together.
The whole world's turned upside down.
What happened to the love we'd found?

Dear Editor,

When will the pain stop?
When do human rights
override the jockeying
for position in the race for
greedy power and elitist privilege?

When will people say,
"What happens to you
will also happen
to those I love
and want to protect"?

When will people say,
"Everyone is valuable
to our community"?

When will service return
as more important than office?

I hope it is soon because
I want the pain on Lopez to stop.
Some say pain makes us stronger.
That is only true for some.
For some it means death—
The death of spirit, heart, mind.
For a child, it can mean the death
of their future dreams because they
lose their sense of personal power.

And the question is always,
"Why do they want
to break the human spirit?"

Please stop the pain
by stopping the greedy,
the destructively powerful,
by stopping those who think
they are the privileged elite
outside of the law and
outside of right action.

Do it at the voting booths.
Be it at the community forums.
Do it with your voice,
your pen, your dollars.
Unify.

Turn your fear
into action.
Make the change.

We are the people
who can stop the pain.
We just need
to do it.

Tender Touch

I need the tender touch of a
Loving someone.
The loving touch, so I can become
A special someone
A touched and loved one.

It's like it's all gone
I know I had it one time
'Cause the feelings are there
And I want to share
It with someone.

It's that song we've
Heard since all of life's begun
Without someone's touch,
What have we won?
It's a song unsung
Like some beads unstrung.

Without the tender touch
Of a loving someone
The loving touch so I can become
A special someone
A special loved one
A touched and fun one . . .
Touching you.

There Came a Day

There came a day
Many years ago
When I finally realized
My way of thinking
Was based on expectations
Of culture, of others.

There came a day
When I finely knew
When clarity rang crystal clear:
Acts are consequential.
Every bill comes due
By myself, of myself.

There came a day
As the light shone bright
Authority is rarely just,
Is mostly for a few.
Ladder paradigms are pressed
Onto neck, into womb.

And on that day,
With understanding
My view of Truth and Justice changed.
The scales fell from my eyes.
For each person's truth is real
In their life, where they live.

And on that day,
I heard Peaceful Truth,
Speak to Justice being served
For all Humanity,
Equally to everyone,
Where they live, where they love.

One Kind of Love

With you it's not skyrockets,
But blue skies and gentle rain.
I like your style, you know.
And you're someplace else to go.

All the time in the world
Is in this very moment.
If only this very moment
Could be all the time in the world.

I like the laugh you laugh
When I tell my jokes to you.
You like my friends,
And they seem to like to be with you.

You're pleasing.
You're easy to talk to.

All the time in the world
Is in this very moment.
If only this very moment,
Could be all the time in the world.

With you here beside me,
It takes up the empty space.
As feelings fold around us,
We are the whole human race.

All the time in the world
Is in this very moment.
If only this very moment,
Could be all the time in the world.

Spirited Children

"Pirates we are
And pirates we'll be.

We'll travel far
Over the sea.

We'll travel by night,
We'll travel by day.

We'll conquer
Everything in our way.
We'll soon be rich
As rich as can be.

Then, we'll travel again,
Over the sea."

***

Brandishing wooden swords.
Wearing newspaper hats.
Gold foil-covered
Chocolate coins
In a wooden chest.

What fun we had
On a sofa ship
With used matchsticks
Stippling mustaches and beards.

Gentle

Gentle touchin', sweet-lovin' man

Haven't you guessed

That you have my heart?

When will you ask for the rest?

Let's wake up together
Inside the early dawn.

You're making dreams
Inside my everyday life.

Lovin' you could fill up the night.

Do my words touch as softly
As my fingers could?

Haven't you guessed
That you have my heart?

When will you ask for the rest?

I Can Almost Believe

Who's gonna get your lovin' tonight?
Who's gonna get
What was dreamed up for you?
Who can I hold
And love and surprise?
As long as I
Don't look in his eyes,
I can almost believe
It's you.

Whose folding arms will hold me in place
While making the
Darkness moist on my face,
Making a kiss
A lingering sigh
As long as I
Don't look in his eyes
I can almost believe
It's you.

Whose smiling face will rest on my breast?
All after the yearning
Is finely gone?
Who will hold me
'Til the crying's done?
As long as I
Don't look in his eyes
I can almost believe
It's you.

Changing from One Place to the Next

Love might bloom from the light.
Contraction and bright expansion
Looms from dark potential
Within the size of a microsecond.

Dreams, quiet, crawl, and cry.
Birth washes forth from what was shy
As The One Sent arrives
Within a mortal capsule.

Forgetting first thing is
As cycles flowing and bursting
Shakes out beasties, flowers
Along with sweet-tasting cake.

No need to conspire,
Feeling from water and fire
Blue, Golds, Burgundy Blush.
Squeezing one world to the next.

Inward Journey

Without anticipation
From the dark belly of a nightmare
Birthed Covid-19.

Drastic measures to survive,
Stuck in the space of isolation
Confines inside time.

Self-reflection companion
Struggles to integrate then and now,
Exploding perceptions.

As the people's needs advance
Holes are punched into classic viewpoints.
Paradigms shatter.

Virus, as catalyst
Puts a mirror to our cultural face,
Waking our action.

Diversity is human
Hearts on fire for justice
As wounds open minds.

Courage strengthens our core
Veils lift and our eyes can see
A new world is here.

Ferry Music 3D

Frothy white caps
Breaking surface,
As whipped-cream crests
Strain and penetrate from
Out of the blue-green.

Moments arrange
The sequence of
Break and bubble
Peak and shadow.

We slide on top
While worlds contrive
Below.

Unaware
Or uncaring
Of islands.

It is an atmosphere
Of liquid domination,
Of earthly matter . . .
And not.

Music is apparent
Quarter notes play out
Among half notes
Staccato and allegro.

Most days
There is no crescendo
So we think the ocean
Is silent

But it continually sings.

Sweet and Fierce Spirituality

Eternal Song

When you find peace of mind
Bring it forth to be.

Bring it like a light that shines
For every heart that's free.

Bring it here.
Bring it now.
Make it loud and long.

Clearly sing to every soul
The true eternal song.

Challenge and Stir

Challenge my mind
Capture my heart;
Most of all,
Stir my soul.

On Lopez Island

The magic seeps into
My bones.
No matter how much I kick
And scream,
The island won't let me
Maintain old ways.

Relaxation sinks in.

At undefended moments,
When I see an eagle,
Or listen to the water
Take possession of the beach,
My own polar shift occurs.

Crazy Notions

Some people see Beauty
Thinking it can be possessed
But this means
Beauty can be suppressed.

These are people who capitalize on Beauty.
They want to own it, use it,
Groom and abuse it. So, they buy it.

Are they trying to fill their own voids?
By owning Beauty?
What is the dividend
Of Beauty?

No one controls Beauty.

It can only be held,
Lovingly,
By Truth.

Only Truth possesses Beauty.
And Truth doesn't want to own it.

Meditation:
Embrace of an Angel

Demanding job, ugly divorce.
Nations butt heads
With threats of war.

So I sit in meditation,
Counting heartbeats to release,
I ask for help.

On back of my eyelids
I see, then feel
A round-shaped floor.

Barely big enough for me,
Walls go straight up
Bending to circular ceiling.

Straining to see
Small opaque top
Confusion, dissonance.

Terror grips mind.
Am I inside a bullet,
Gasping, a small missile?

Glimpsing a face
Lifting up as
Walls spread outward.

Diffuse pastels
Spread through sides
And out bigger with wings.

Colors vibrate
Inside me as they move,
Erasing fear.

Truth revealed
No bullet, no missile,
Only the embrace
Of an angel.

If

If we are to love our sisters and brothers
Do we need to love ourselves?

As we love ourselves,
Do we not realize the love of
And the loving for all?

As we accept this love
Is it not a natural thing
To also love our home, the Earth?

To feel the community of people
And rocks and soil
And trees and birds?

Which one of us will reflect
This first to a brother or sister?

Questioning Uncle About World War II

"Have the people been fed?"

"Find your own place, Brenda."

"I want my space, I care.
Are our people cared for?"

"The baggage is heavy.
Wisdom comes from surviving."

"I have survived."

"Sometimes the present
Looks like the past.
Wisdom means you have hope
For the better.
Everything is real and alive
With joy and pain."

"Is there smoke coming from the furnace, yet?
What do the marks on the wall mean, Uncle?"

"Hate, prejudice, greed
Decadence, fear . . .
Great sorrow."

"Uncle, Do you
remember
the end of the war?"

"I remember the
end of the world."

Seduction

Like a spider
Spinning a golden web,
Reaching out with beautiful crystal thread.
Offering broken bread
With magic curves,
A new thought
Serves my mind.

I can't escape this alchemy,
Like fighting back a memory.

Like a circle
Bending 'round my head.
Dance me 'round your
Wond'rous silver bed.
Balancing on the edge.
In mystic shades
He promenades for me.

Draw me in, I can't resist.
A dark angel's kiss.

Like inside some
Old and familiar song,
Catch me up to
Where I know I belong.
Never mind right or wrong.
You're whispering again.
I'm giving in to you.

Alpha, Omega

You are Beginning and Ending,
Alpha, Omega, the All.

Myself is the flowing
Returning and growing,
And always is part of the Whole.

You are the ocean
As I am a wave
And the water flows through,
All is One.

As I was and will be, You are.

As I stir a flower,
It troubles a star.

These are the first, the middle, the last.
These are the parts of the whole.

If we can grasp just what we are,
We're the body, the spirit, the soul.

We Have Been Called

We have been called,
By a resurrection of life
That is beyond all culture.

We have been called
By a quantum leap
Of body and mind change.

We have been called
To kill arrogance
Before it kills the child.

We have been called
To serve God, Earth,
And Humankind.

We have been called.

WoW

Women of Wisdom,
Authentic power.
Seeking ways to express.
A new genesis
Re-establishing
A circle of wisdom.

Multifaceted,
From many perspectives,
They arc, connect, and reflect.

Then, they separate
To follow individual paths
Coming from each heart
And mind
In unity of purpose.

Each their own, Unto their own.
Much love and energy
Will make the walls fall down
As the energy moves out.

A three-degree curve
Gathers those who
See and participate
In the Holy Truth.

Will walls of rigidity fall at their feet?

Make way!
Allow auto-reaction to
Encompass compassion
With resolve to commence.

Call out the bully
In a fight without fists.
Supreme priorities for survival,
Bliss is riding the steed of Justice.

Strengthening boundaries
Within compassion
Starts with the smaller details.

Excite the potential
With the movement of fire.
State, form, time
Become formless again.
To spiral something new
For women of wisdom
For all the children
Creating a better future.

Mary's Tears

A sacredness touches me,
quietly signals me,
"Be relaxed."

Shifting shapes form
From watery emotion
And fiery passion . . .
Spreading . . .
Seeking wisdom
From the heart,
To dance with insight.

Muted by a lumpy throat,
It spills abundantly
From eyes
Salty and blood-soaked.

Christ's symbols
Of blood and water.
Mary adds salt
Testing for truth.

I know why Mary cries.
I know why Mary silently cries.

"God counts every tear of a woman";
An old Kabbalah saying.
What truth of honoring
Is spoken here?
Why is the truth
Not spoken by a woman?

Are there tears
For Mary
Of Magdala?
Labeled whore
Instead of spiritual daughter,
Instead of first apostle.

As energy
Is of womankind's
Natural connectedness,
Power and fear are part
Of mankind's present path.

The revolution of Earth time
May take us back
To the Garden
For a new plan.

How long,
Sweet Mother,
How long?

She cries:
For the loss
Of the celebration
Of divinity in women.

Does the salt in the tears
Make the pain immaculate?

Or is the truth of the pain
Only felt more fully
In an immaculate heart?

Child abuse alone
Would break a mother's heart
And bring the tears.

His story broke the fierceness
Of a mother who protects her children.
It is in the Divine Mother.

She cries:
Can only male divinity
Express with Word?

Does the kiss give life or voice?
Does it open the throat?
Does that bring up the pain . . .
Or does it bring up the strength?

Is it time for an immaculate heart to be within a warrior?

She cries
For those who say they honor the male
While they destroy the feminine
In each and every man and woman.

How can there be a Father without a Mother?

Greenman

Painting.
Intending an angel.
Praying for St. Michael
And his protection.

Side face view of
Curved beard
Leafy petals for
Hair and face.

A Greenman.

Energy of
Angels and faeries.
Six limbs.
Four like humans
Plus two wings.

No wings for Greenman
But a spirit, guardian
Of nature
And natural processes.

One from three.
They all work with
Creation.
Perhaps,
The efficacious activity,

Potent intensity
Whether quiet or thunderous,
Keeps humanity on track.

Hope

In today's world
Of toxins, climate change, genetic changes
With nowhere to run,
How do we have hope?

When threads of life
Are interwoven with some kind
Of "family" or community theme,
Then we feel confident about our future.

Uniting serves
As a balm for the anxiety
In our times.

Perhaps,
We can reach for that
In the sounds of happy children
And the smells and sights of nature.
Happy children means healthy children.
Seeing happy children
Along with the sights and smells of nature
Are most certainly instigators of hope.

We can survive anything
If we can experience
Motivators for hope.
Moving towards hope,
We can perceive a future.

We must work towards a future
That supports healthy and happy children.
We must work together
To intend a better environment
For the unseen future.

Unity is needed.

We must unite across religion,
Gender, class status, ethnicity,
And across all false boundaries.

People from all walks of life,
All gender orientations,
From all economies,
And across all age groups
Will work to change our culture
For all children's sake.

We will weep together
In sorrow for what's lost
And with tears of joy
For what is coming.

Conversation Between Our Lady And Our Lord

"Sweet Lord,
The Light cannot be seen without the Dark.
I can only bring the Light to Our Children
By showing The Darkness."

"Beautiful Lady, then bring on The Darkness.
Without Truth, there can be no Justice.
Without Light, is there Truth?
If they cannot see the Light,
Then bring on the Darkness."

"Blessed Be, My Lord.
We are Unified for Our Children!
Together, We will do this with Love.
They will need
All the support we can give them
To survive
What they must go through
To see The Light."

"Yes, Sweet and Dearest Heart,
Show Our Children.
Our Compassion
Will support them to Love Each and the Other.
They will learn the Power of Their own Kindness."

"And the Circle will break their hearts open
And grow and become a Spiral."

"We'll salute Our Children with a Dance, Shall We?"

"Oh, yes, My Love, with The Dance of Life!"

Dimming

The moon bares her ample face.
The sun releases his warmth.
I hide my heart and
Steal away into the dark
To cover my soul.

We all ride the Milky Way
Waiting 'til the next big bang
While silky Cygnus swims
And spreads her wings,
Ancient wisdom slides
Into dimming secret past.

Prayers

Where I Have Sunk

Where I have sunk,
Drowning in darkness,
May kindness find me.

Where I have sat
At peace with darkness
to understand,
Help me to stay calm.

Where past hurts fester,
Show me openness
To all Beloved.
Let me be a force
For your Word.

Amen.

God-Shine

When I hear a word of anger
Help me to be a friend and a neighbor
And let the God-shine through

Let me shine back your light
In the darkness
Let me hold up your love
To the world
Let me shine back your light
In the darkness
Let me be a force
For your Word.

When a friend has grief or worry
Help me to listen with my heart
And let the God-shine through.

When I see someone in trouble
Help me show His life's
A better way
And let the God-shine through.

Let me shine back your light
In the darkness
Let me hold up your love
To the world
Let me shine back your light
In the darkness
And let the God-shine through.

When

When I am at peace
I connect with you from within.

When I am distressed
I've noticed you reach for me from without.

When I'm consumed with my fear or worry,
You send someone to reach me.

When I'm lost, it is all in my perspective
Because you are without, within,
and working through others.

Amen.

Merciful Source

O, Merciful Source of All,
Take pity on those
Who have no one to lean on
When they are weak.

Who have no one to feed them
When they are hungry,
Who have no one to shelter them,
When they are cold.

Please open our eyes.
We'll hold them in our hearts
So we can offer
A morsel of food,
A kindness,
A place to shelter.

And for those
Who have it all
But have lost their way,
Please take pity
And open their minds and hearts.

Blessed Be.

Honor Great Mother

Great Mother, I honor You
By honoring all living things.

May the Earth know
I respect Her
Abundance and sustenance
Given to all generations.

Bless us
So our eyes see
As our heart is unsealed.

Show us the path
To make a true, honest
Relationship with
All creation.

Blessed Be.

For the Altar

Sweet and joyful
Source of Life,
Send angels to help me
Through this time of conflict,
This time of desperation,
This time of gnawing stress.

The beginning and ending
Of all there is
Is in Creation.
Is where I dwell with You within.

Help me find the
Path of peace as
I put it All on the Altar
And give All to Thee.

Blessed Be.

Mother-Father God

Mother-Father God

Bones of the Mother
Rays of the Father
Earth and Sky

Enrich us with the Wisdom to know and
To love you.
Test us to strengthen us so we stand
For what is right.

Enfold us with enough of your Love
So we understand
How we are to
Love one another.

Blessed Be.

O Great Source

O Great Source
Of all life and death cycles
Of everything male, female, both, and neither

Of all things unjudged for value
Of all things humans possess or judge

Set our footsteps on a path
That supplicates our actions
In renewal of all life processes
Whether deemed living or nonliving.
To support life for all
All people, all living things,

Amen.

Hold My Loved Ones

Please hold my loved ones
When I cannot.
Please comfort their furrowed minds
If all seems lost,
If they are alone.
When there is no respite.

Please hold my loved ones
When they have troubles.
Please relieve their trembling limbs
If they cannot
Stand in what is truth
And justice is gone.

Please hold my loved ones
If they're abandoned.
Please kiss the pain from their souls
If they see not
Kindness from others
Nor Your countenance.

Amen.

What Shines from Others

Support hope in us
That we may move
Away from fear
To defeat those forces
We cannot change.

The You that shines from others.

Make our eyes clear
So we can see
The You that is in others
And see their true spirit
Reflecting You to us.

The You that shines from others.

Support our soul connections
That we may move
Away from anger
And towards

The You that shines from others.

Acknowledgements

Special thanks to: Wendy and Aaron Stephenson and children; Sandy Coakley; John Waugh; Jedidiah Smith; Patti McCormick; Lopez Island Public Library; San Juan County Library Writers' Group; Red Wheelbarrow Writers' Group; Cami Ostman; Lisa Dailey at Sidekick Press, Bellingham; Karen Imler; Georgia McDade; Sally Hedges-Blanquez; Raul Sanchez; David Rose; Kay Frances; Pablo Paz; among many others.

Special thank you to both my parents, Rosemary C. Allison and Thomas R. Asterino, for their encouragement from childhood, and to my Aunt Audrey Waddington Cox and Mary Elizabeth Astorino. I am grateful to the strong women in front of me and the strong women behind me (Rosemary, Mabel, Sarah, Elizabeth, Elizabeth, Sally, Mary, and Esther). And to the women who stand beside me, I am eternally in your debt.

Photo by Rick Wigre

Brenda Asterino lives on Lopez Island, Washington, where she volunteers with the local independent radio station, KLOI-LP 102.9 FM, as a producer. She also volunteers with the American Red Cross. Asterino worked as a private and public educator for nearly twenty-five years when life was forever changed by a car accident. Her education includes an AA in Humanities, BS in Biology, and MA in Education, along with many years of training in parapsychology, Energy Work and Body Work.

With *Pathways* being her second poetry publication, Consciousness is an overriding theme that intertwines and entangles all aspects of everything. Genealogy seems to be an area that will support many people's ideas about themselves. In hoping that we all find we have shared so much of all human stories, may we all rejoice in our shared struggles and insights. Asterino supports nonviolent environmental activism, appreciation of diversity of cultures and humanity, and hopes for unity of everyone for the health and well-being of all children everywhere.

CPSIA information can be obtained
at www.ICGtesting.com
Printed in the USA
FSHW010711071021
85266FS